YOUR DAUGHTER'S COUNTRY

JOHN DORSEY

~

BLUE HORSE PRESS REDONDO BEACH, CALIFORNIA 2019

YOUR DAUGHTER'S COUNTRY

JOHN DORSEY

Blue Horse Press
318 Avenue I # 760
Redondo Beach,
California   90277

Cover art: Jeffrey C. Alfier,
"Abandoned Farmstead, Lincoln County, New Mexico"

Editors: Jeffrey and Tobi Alfier
Blue Horse Press logo: Amy Lynn Hayes (1996)

ISBN 978-0-578-46459-6

꙰

for emilie rose dorsey & frank t. rios

Contents

Foreword

All work was completed at The Osage Arts Community in Belle, Missouri. Grateful thanks is given to Mark McClane & Tony Hayden for their continued generous support.

FOREWORD

The running joke is that if you ever find yourself the subject of one of John Dorsey's poems, things will not end well for you. But the truth of the matter is this: if you ever find yourself the subject of one of John Dorsey's poems, he loves you. He loves us all in our broken lives that never quite turn out the way we planned. He loves our beat up and rusted-out cars, the dive bars and chicken joints which are the only places we can really afford even though settling the tab always brings on that discernible stab of anxiety. John Dorsey loves the people about whom Eliot or Stevens or Plath or Oliver would never write.

In Dorsey's world, everyone deserves his love and he gives it to them freely. He knows that they will disappoint. He knows that, all things being equal, people will make bad decisions, but he loves them anyway. He loves their stories, their small triumphs, their failures, their ability to get up and do it again, and, sometimes, he loves them when they don't know when to stay down. He loves them even when they can't get up again. He loves their bad reputations, both earned and unwarranted. He loves them in their big, imperfect, unidyllic and brutally honest truth.

Because outside of the perfectly scripted fiction of the American Dream, John Dorsey is there writing poems about the people who can't Horatio Alger themselves out of their bad day. Or their bad years. Or their bad lives. He writes in such bare language that the only thing left is raw and open and bruised.

But Dorsey sees the beauty in these lives, too: the fry cook who dances to Prince and makes kisses with her lips, Emilie Rose who "got married / raised a family / & talked to the dead." He chronicles the lives of his subjects with an impartial journalist's eye and pen. If he were a photographer, Dorsey's subjects would be off center, off balance, and blurred just a little in grainy black and white. But I bet most of them would be smiling.

If you're reading this, you're holding a copy of *Your Daughter's Country*. Turn the page. You'll know what I mean.

Shawn Pavey
February 13, 2019

Poem for Olin Marshall

all my grandmother's cousin ever wanted
was his own pizza & a used lawn tractor
the son of sharecroppers & war heroes
he drove a school bus & raised wild dogs
that bit the hand that fed them
he sat outside by the fire
talking about his dead sister
as if she were a saint

she had been gone since 1973
the same year his wife passed
& he still had never seen a ghost
quite as lovely

his younger brother had been a race car driver
just before the second world war
when he crashed & burned
he left him a small fortune
that was still sitting in the bank
nearly half a century later

on his birthday we convinced him
to get the tractor
but the pizza still felt
like an extravagance

he would just gaze out at his property
in front of the old family general store
spitting dried up chewing tobacco
into a rusted coffee can
harvesting sunlight
without lifting a finger
gathering his history up like dead leaves
like a pile of bones

if the wind had any sense of mercy
it would've taken him too.

A History of Bite Marks

olin's dog bruno
would bite anything
that came near him

when a bat soared past my aunt's ear
as she tried to get some sleep
in the bed of my grandfather's truck
he leaped toward it
like he was chasing a firefly
in the cold west virginia evening

when my grandmother got a new dog
olin offered my cousin amanda & i
2 bucks to wash them both off
in the creek up the way
that was full of cow shit

he nearly tore the poor thing's ear clean off
as they wrestled in the dirty water

he tried to take chunks out of our ankles
if we tried to bathe outside
or sit by the fire
or breathe overly loudly
for any prolonged period
of time.

Walking After Midnight in Linn, Missouri
for jeanette powers

it's the middle of the afternoon
& the jukebox that once offered
a youthful kiss from patsy cline in the moonlight
is now drowned out by the bartender
talking about how the fry cook
is not her boyfriend

sleepy eyed construction workers
are left to dream about true love
on their own as they wander back out
into the cold

their regrets will haunt them
long after the grease
from the fried chicken special
has settled in their stomachs

settling is just the way of things
nobody is searching for anyone
after midnight here

pride only makes you lonely

while the rest of the world
is fast asleep.

In Front of Magic Mike's

we watch from the window
as a drunk driver in a rusted-out silver pickup
clips the side of a parked school bus
in front of magic mike's

thankfully nobody is hurt
though a fireman slips in the mud
leftover after a january ice storm

everything is melted
the driver is screaming at the county sheriff
about just wanting to go home

the former mayor looks like he needs a nap
as he tries to put the mailbox back in the ground
while they take her away in cuffs.

Poem for J.P.

i don't know how many pairs of glasses you lost
how many retainers fell off lunch trays
never to be seen again

these are myths we rarely speak of now

like the ketchup packages we used to launch
off cafeteria tables
that would sail through the air
& land in the hoodies
of other unsuspecting kids

the last time i saw you
it should have been snowing
your own son sat beside you in a booth coloring
while struggling to finish his chicken fingers
even with your help

your laugh was sincere
but you looked tired
for the first time
in over 30 years

talking about your own father
& the tent we used to sleep in
in your backyard

& your mother's pinto
with its rusted-out passenger side
where you had to hold your feet up
while driving to the grocery store
as if you were in an episode of the flintstones
it all feels a bit like time travel now
it's almost like it happened to someone else
better versions of ourselves
who would always burn longer
than the sun.

Wolfgang

was raised by his grandfather
on a barren patch of dirt
just up the street from my bus stop
in high school he dated a girl
with thick glasses & a mouth like a dying volcano
who worked second shift with my mom
at the local wendy's

they'd scream at each other
& then make up
just as loudly
behind the dumpster
out back

after graduation rehearsal
we went out into the woods
to smoke a joint
when he told me
that last summer she'd been pregnant
until he threw her down the stairs
but that it was really for the best

he had a short temper & a long bloodline

the trees made him feel small
like he was drowning in a inch of bathwater
& that he would've left already
if he could.

Caroline Haiku

your skin is a nervous yellow
like a dying sunflower
in the toledo morning.

Coco Malone is a Bad Bitch
for jen dayton

before jen moved to brooklyn
she had spent the summer on robinwood
drinking red wine & squealing in italian
everytime her boyfriend
ran his hands down her back

telling us all about rome
how it made her feel
like a different person

the sun felt different
her heart felt different
her dreams felt unexplainable

fear had become an inextinguishable fight song
she had to commit to canvas

she was more than one thing
more than one place

she was a dark corner
on cherry street
in the bowery

she said coco malone
would only come out at night
she was a bad bitch

she said they would only dance together
for a few heated seconds

that she was both of them
in a screaming match with herself

that you could never be sure
which one would greet you
in the morning.

Toledo Girls

bridget can't walk without shaking
but i still love her
caroline smells like rose petals
& southern comfort
but i still love her
jessica can't have children
but i still love her
tall jen has multiple personalities now
& i love all of them equally
little jenni isn't whole without a bottle of wine
but i still love her
sarah jayne won't stay in one place
long enough to let me love her
but i still love her.

The End of the Line

my dad's uncle dave would sit in his bedroom
rolling cigarettes & talking to truckers
on his hand built crystal radio
he was always that friendly voice
on the other end of the line

his universe was a long haul
on a short wave

when he went out
he'd check payphones for quarters
everywhere he went
& wipe out arcade claw machines
with a surgeon's steady grip
selling stuffed animals & worthless trinkets
at the flea market every sunday

he taught me how to build my own radio
from a $6 kit i bought
at the local electronics store
because i wanted to talk to the dead

cleopatra
napoleon
billy the kid
lee harvey oswald
liberace
lawrence welk

they were all still out there somewhere
listening for signs of life
in western pennsylvania

when my great aunt leona lay dying
in a hospital bed tossing & turning
as it rained outside her window
all she wanted was to see him again
to have him hold her hand
through the fog of silence
to hear his voice
rolling down the highway
toward anyone
who would listen.

Birthday Poems for the Dead

for frank t. rios

it's always your birthday now

this isn't a poem for the dead

they wouldn't get it

refuse anything they offer you

& help me light another candle

love is holding out for more.

Your Daughter's Country

my grandmother's father
once owned hundreds of acres of land
teeming with corn & cattle
tobacco & a dozen children that he left behind
just after the depression hit
he met my great grandmother
working as a ranch hand for her father
somewhere in west virginia or pennsylvania

the family history gets a little fuzzy

it wasn't until i was in my 20's
that i found out that he had also been
an alcoholic
a railroad man
& a rapist

something my own father never even knew

forced by her father to stay put
after she got pregnant
bearing him several more children
who looked like the milkman
the postal carrier
the trash collector
any one of them made for better company
on a cold night
as he was off riding the rails

they never married
but after he died
they gave her a pass
to ride the train
anywhere she wanted

she never used it

it all seemed like dark country
with its abandoned children
left like tumbleweeds
grasping at straws
for their own mongrel bloodline

there was never anywhere for her to go

that was far enough away
from where she'd already been.

My Grandmother's Half Sister

lived less than a mile
from where we'd vacation
when i was a kid

i only ever met her the once
her skin was cracked
from hours spent
in the blazing sun

i liked to pretend she was a lizard
as she sipped a glass
of home brewed sweet tea

her mouth was shaped like china
commemorating the dust bowl

her teeth almost seemed
to blow away in the breeze
every time she laughed.

Aunt Mary

my uncle jerry
lived with the same woman
for over 20 years
without ever giving her a ring

she had a tenth grade education
& a laugh like a hyena

she would eat $20 worth of burger king
as long as it came with a diet coke
& threatened to stab any woman
who looked in his direction

every time i would walk
into my grandparents house
my grandfather would laugh & say
aren't you happy to see your aunt mary?

i would just glance in her direction
& then quickly look away
before her daggers had a chance
to stab me too.

We Were Still Brave Then

when my grandfather was laid off
in the winter of 1986
my cousin amanda & i stayed up
with flashlights under a blanket
counting our money

a whole $8 between us
we stuffed it into an envelope
& put it on the kitchen table downstairs
with a note written with a dull crayola crayon
about how we just wanted to help out

now i get scared
when my bank account
dips below $100

thinking about toledo
when i wouldn't eat
for 3 or 4 days at a time

but we were braver then
when anything over $5
seemed like it could solve
all of the world's problems

in the morning
my grandfather hugged both of us
before giving us our money back

a few days later
the space shuttle challenger exploded
fast & furious & brilliant
& as i went outside
majesty just seemed
to turn into dirty snow
& even the stars
seemed to have
their limits.

Poem for Mary Anthony

mary says that you won't find god
in the stacks of books
we have piled high
in the bookstore in town

she was a trucker
before she moved back
to open up the only motel for miles
all that time on the highway
if she couldn't find him
out under the stars
what chance do we have?

Gasconade Haiku

the sun is a radical lover
a racist moon
turned pale.

First Impressions of Belle, Missouri

as a kid
my cousin & i spent summers in a trailer
in west virginia
with no running water

we would bathe in the sunlight
in a large steel drum
used to feed cattle in the 1930's

there was no valor in poverty

there were no ghost stories
about dead indians buried in the hills

i had to come here
for that.

Tommy

my great uncle tommy
was born with cerebral palsy
just like me

one of the sweetest men
i've ever known
he was a large baby
big enough to swallow
whole japanese tourists
in some infant godzilla scenario

while i was the size of a minnow
so small they almost threw me back

the only boy
he never left his mother's side
until the day
they put her in the ground
& he spelled her name out in rose petals
on a cheap pine box
that held all the family secrets.

The War at Home

as my aunt victoria kicked around
in my grandmother's stomach
the war raged in vietnam
& boys like my father
waited by the mailbox
for death sentences.

His Summer Place

my grandfather's side business painting houses
went south just long enough
for him to lose a piece of property
that had been in our family
since the turn of the century

it was supposed to be his summer place
even though he worked
no matter what season it was

he always said
you have to stay busy

you can't paint
the town red
without a little blood.

White Castle on New Year's
for alex nielsen

i gave alex my last $6
when he offered to go
on a food run just after 3 am

an hour later he came back
covered in fresh bruises & soiled snow
telling me he'd been jumped
by a couple of guys
on the way home

he said they took his money
his french fries & his crave case
of pulled pork sliders

but that he'd managed to hide
my bag of chicken rings
deep inside his bookbag

they were soggy
& tasted like heartburn
& the desperation of winter
along collingwood blvd
but we tapped two together anyway
as if they were filet mignon
& cheersed to another new year
in toledo.

Dressing a Deer in Yellow Springs, Ohio
for jeff west

jessica kept complaining
about wanting taco bell
until we got in jeff's car
in the middle of the night
5 or 6 stoned college girls
piled high on top of each other
in the back seat

jeff turned on his headlights
& we heard a sudden thud
noticing a bleeding deer
attempting to run
into the treeline before collapsing

all of the girls started screaming
i covered my ears
& jeff just stopped the car
popped the trunk & got out
coming back with a shotgun
to finish it off

he threw the deer & the gun
back in the trunk

A few miles down the road
we ordered tacos in silence
& headed back to their dorm
where jeff made squeamish vegan girls
help him carry in the lifeless thing
to the nearest sink still dripping blood
he taught them how to dress a fresh kill
later making venison stew
while everyone else
quietly ate their burritos.

Belle the Musical

in the dining room of the dinner belle
everyone gives love a bad name
waitresses & camouflage covered farmers
shout out bon jovi lyrics
like they're reciting hamlet

he never went through anything
like the struggles
they face every day

in the kitchen
the cook flours
a small mountain of chicken
before throwing it into the fryer
& shakes her ass
as prince comes on the radio
stopping every few seconds
to make a kissing sound
with her lips.

Poem for Larry Gawel

it's hard to find a direct positive
for thin skin
in a fair weather town

history is unpredictable

religion is a hitching post
for comfort food

this town has a sign that says
get settled in.

What's Left of Love
for Mark Shaffer

isn't buried in a flower garden
in your backyard
or on the lips of a minister
who couldn't get your wife's name right
through the entire service.

On Water Street

as we sat in the diner
across from my friend terry's old studio
counting out loose change
to pay for a single plate of toast & eggs
they found a body floating behind the building

ask anyone
it's sink or swim in north toledo
even if all you're trying to do
is cross the river styx
one final lap
at a time.

When Terry was in Rescue Crisis

there was this guy
who claimed to have been
on star search in the winter of 1984
just like in life
nobody ever remembers
the runner up

instead they ask you
for your last cigarette

before you wander off
to a better time.

Me & Bobby McGee

for kris kristofferson & caroline gauger

i'm sure that song
was written for a girl in toledo

with fiery red hair
who sang you to sleep
on a warm summer night.

Dean

my dad's cousin dean
could raise his lip
like elvis presley

he was the king
of western pennsylvania
but couldn't sing a lick.

From Memory

after my grandfather went blind
he had my grandmother
take him to get
his driver's license renewed

& snuck out to his truck
as fast as his prosthetic leg
would carry him

somehow he got in
& drove into town from memory

& right off the side of a little bridge
& into the icy cold creek water

the policeman who found him
just had the family come take him home
without reporting anything

on the way there he remembered
how he used to shoot from the foul line
& danced circles around those jokers
at his high school prom

now he had to do everything
from memory.

Poem for Oscar on a Life Well Lived

my great uncle oscar
was named after his father
who dropped dead
of a heart attack at the age of 52
just after the second world war

he drove stock cars at the local track
well into his 80's
& when he laughed
his love for his wife
showed all of his face.

River People
for andrew tucker

our people come from the hills of shenandoah
& the rivers of pittsburgh

if you've ever seen a paper sailboat
burn up from the inside

then you know trash flows evenly
no matter where you throw it

dirty water is dirty water.

Andrew

i wonder if my grandmother looked like you
i wonder if i have your eyes or your nose
i wonder if you ever rode the same rails
where neal cassady watched his final sunset
with a bottle in his hand.

The Ballad of Emilie Rose

your life wasn't exactly a sad song
you got married
raised a family
& talked to the dead
through the mouths of butterflies
who promised to never fly away.

About the Author

John Dorsey has been writing poetry since the late 1980's and has been involved in the publishing community for more than two decades. He is the author of around 50 books and chapbooks, a few of the more recent being ***Being the Fire* (Tangerine Press, 2016)** and ***Shoot the Messenger* (Red Flag Press, 2017),** the latter was funded by Indiana University of Pennsylvania's English Department. An 11-time Pushcart Prize nominee, his work has appeared more than 2,000 magazines and anthologies from around the world. He has read or spoken at colleges and universities such as the University of Toledo, Assumption College, Cleveland State University, Seton Hill University, University of the Arts, Erie Community College, Southeast Missouri State University, Indiana University of Pennsylvania, the University of Missouri-St. Louis, The University of Pittsburgh at Greensburg, and Missouri University of Science & Technology, as well as other assorted venues such as the The Walt Whitman Birthplace, The Bowery Poetry Club and Beyond Baroque . For several years he served as a judge for the Arts Commission of Greater Toledo's Art in Tarta Project, which chose poems to be presented on city transit buses. In 2006, he won the Toledo City Paper's annual poetry and fiction competition, and would go on to serve as a judge the following year, before being named the city's Best Literary Artist in their 2014 reader poll. In 2010, he also served as a judge for Grievous Jones Press' Grievous Prize issued in Cardiff, Wales, and in 2013 for the Standing Rock Cultural Arts Open Chapbook Competition in Kent, Ohio. From 2003-2012, he served as an Artist-in-Residence at the Collingwood Arts Center in Toledo, Ohio and in 2015, Dorsey was awarded a Visiting Artist Residency by the Osage Arts Community in Belle, MO, where he currently resides. In 2017 he received a two appointment to serve as Belle's first city Poet Laureate from Mayor Steve Vogt and has gone on to found the city's first literary publication the **Gasconade Review,** which he edits with Jason Ryberg. He is a graduate of the University of Arts' Writing for Film and Television program, completing his education there in 2002. In 2017 he served as the subject for a poetry documentary by NYC filmmaker Carson Parish. He may be reached at archerevans@yahoo.com.